Riccardo Bozzi

THE WORLD BELONGS TO YOU

illustrated by Olimpia Zagnoli

templar books
an imprint of Candlewick Press

The world belongs to you.

And you belong to the world.

You are free.

Hopefully.

You are free.

But you have limits.

You are free to believe
in anything you want.

You are also free
to believe in nothing at all.

You are free to love anyone you want.

You are free to let love go.

You are free to be loved.

Or not.

You are free
to play.

And play
and play
and play.

You are free to learn.

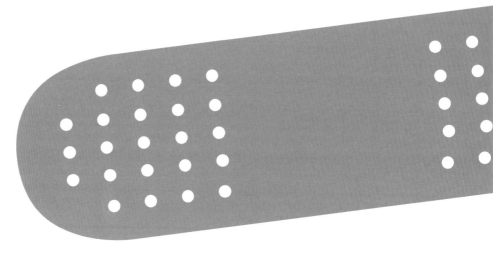

Even though it might hurt sometimes.

You are free to be happy.

But it won't always be easy.

You are free to be unhappy.

Which isn't usually very hard.

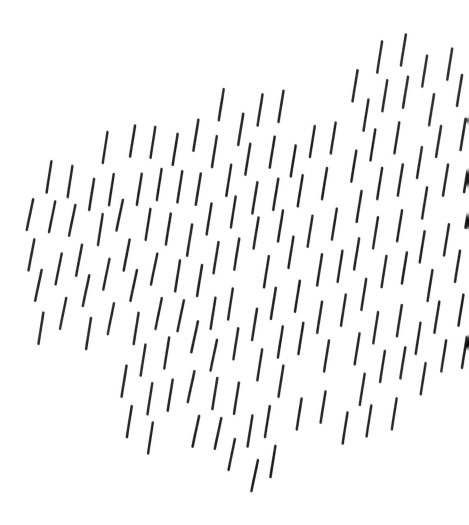

As strange as it seems,
being unhappy isn't useless.

Quite the opposite.

You are free,
but you have limits.

And yet you are free
to overcome these limits.

Because the world belongs to you.

And you belong to the world.

First U.S. edition 2013

Library of Congress Catalog Card Number
2012942658
ISBN 978-0-7636-6488-6

TTP 17 16 15 14 13 12
10 9 8 7 6 5 4 3 2 1

Printed in Huizhou, Guangdong, China

This book was typeset in Univers LT Std.
The illustrations were created digitally.

Designed by Bunker
Produced by Templar Publishing

TEMPLAR BOOKS

an imprint of Candlewick Press
99 Dover Street
Somerville, Massachusetts 02144
www.candlewick.com

This book is dedicated to
the Busy Bee and the Mighty Mouse.